NumPy

In 8 Hours

For Beginners

Learn Coding Fast

Ray Yao

About This Book

"NumPy Programming" is a textbook for high school and college students; it covers all essential NumPy language knowledge. You can learn complete primary skills of NumPy programming fast and easily.

The textbook includes a lot of practical examples for beginners and includes exercises for the college final exam, the engineer certification exam, and the job interview exam.

"NumPy Programming" is a useful textbook for beginners. The straightforward definitions, the plain examples, the elaborate explanations and the neat layout feature this helpful and educative book. You will be impressed by its distinctive and tidy writing style. Reading this book is a great enjoyment!

Note

This book is only suitable for programming beginners, high school students and college students; it is not for the experienced programmers.

Prerequisite to Learn NumPy

Before learning the NumPy, you should have basic knowledge of Python programming.

Kindle Books by Ray Yao

C# Cheat Sheet

C++ Cheat Sheet

JAVA Cheat Sheet

JavaScript Cheat Sheet

PHP MySQL Cheat Sheet

Python Cheat Sheet

Html Css Cheat Sheet

Linux Command Line

Paperback Books by Ray Yao

C# Cheat Sheet

C++ Cheat Sheet

JAVA Cheat Sheet

JavaScript Cheat Sheet

PHP MySQL Cheat Sheet

Python Cheat Sheet

Html Css Cheat Sheet

Linux Command Line

(Each Cheat Sheet contains more than 300 examples, more than 300 outputs, and more than 300 explanations.)

Table of Contents

Hour 1

Prerequisite to learn NumPy

Before learning the NumPy, you should have basic knowledge of Python and the array, because NumPy works with Python and arrays.

What is NumPy?

NumPy (Numerical Python) is an open source extension of Python Numerical computation. This tool can be used to store and process large matrices. It is much more efficient than Python's own nested list structure. It supports multiple dimensional array and matrix operations. In addition, it also provides a large number of mathematical libraries for array operations. NumPy is used for working with arrays.

Humpy's predecessor, Numeric was originally developed by Jim Holguin and other collaborators. In 2005, they developed successfully NumPy in Numeric by combining the features of another generic library, Numeracy, and adding other extensions. At last, NumPy forms a kind of open source code and is maintained and developed by many collaborators together.

Python itself has lists and arrays, but for large data processing, its structures have a number of drawbacks. Python does not support the multiple dimensional arrays and matrixes very well, therefore NumPy fills these gaps, and it provides two basic objects: Narre and Funk, which are suitable for numeric calculation of such kind of data. In short, NumPy is a Python library.

What is NumPy for?

NumPy can help you study:

1. Data science or machine learning

2. Linear algebraic integral interpolation, special functions.

3. Signal processing and image processing.

4. Scientific and Engineering Computing

5. Ordinary differential equation

6. Provide an application program interface (API)

Prerequisite to learn NumPy

Before you learn NumPy programming, you must have the knowledge of the Python language.

Install NumPy

1. Before installing NumPy, you need to install the latest version Python to your local computer. The Python download link is:

https://www.python.org/

2. Having downloaded the Python installer, you can install Python.

3. After installing Python, please restart your computer.

4. Test the Python. Please click:

Window System > Command Prompt > Input the following command:

C:\User\YourName>python

```
C:\Users\RAY>python
Python 3.9.4 (tags/v3.9.4:1f2e308, Apr
Type "help", "copyright", "credits" or
>>>
```

5. If you can see the Python version, it means that Pathos have installed successfully.

6. The command to install NumPy is:

```
C:\User\YourName>pip install numpy
```

7. Please click:

Window System > Command Prompt > Input the following command:

C:\User\YourName>pip install numpy

```
C:\Users\RAY>pip install numpy
```

8. After install NumPy, you can see:

```
C:\Users\RAY>pip install numpy
Collecting numpy
  Downloading numpy-1.20.2-cp39-cp39-w
  :
Installing collected packages: numpy
Successfully installed numpy-1.20.2
```

9. Congratulation! NumPy has been installed successfully!

Set Up Python Editor

We need to set up Python first so that it can work as a NumPy editor.

1. Please click:

Python3.9 > IDLE (Python 3.9 64-bit) > open the Python editor.

2. Please click:

Options > Configure IDLE > General > Open Edit Window > OK.

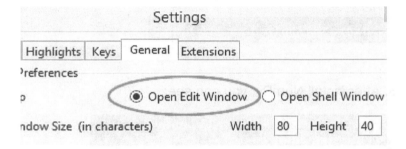

3. Restart the Python/NumPy Editor.

Congratulation! You can easily edit your NumPy program by using this editor from now on.

Import NumPy Library

Before we run the NumPy program, we need to import NumPy library.

```
import numpy
```

Example 1.1

```
import numpy
myArr = numpy.array([0, 1, 2, 3, 4, 5])
print(myArr)
```

Output:

[0 1 2 3 4 5]

Explanation:

"import numpy" is a NumPy command, which is used to import NumPy library into the current program first.

Alias of NumPy Library

We usually use "np" as the alias of the NumPy library.

The syntax to define an "np" is as follows:

```
import numpy as np
```

Example 1.2

```
import numpy as np
myArr = np.array([0, 1, 2, 3, 4, 5])
print(myArr)
```

Output:

[0 1 2 3 4 5]

Explanation:

"import numpy as np" defines an "np" as the alias of the NumPy library.

NumPy Array

Two syntaxes to create a NumPy array are:

myArray = np.array([v1, v2, v3, …])	# the first syntax
myArray = np.arange(v1, v2)	# the second syntax

arange(v1, v2) returns the numbers from the v1 to the v2 -1.

E.g. arange(1, 5) returns 1, 2, 3, 4

Example 1.3

```
import numpy as np
arr1 = np.array([0, 1, 2, 3, 4, 5])
print(arr1)
arr2 = np.arange( 0, 6 )    # not include 6
print(arr2)
```

Output:

[0 1 2 3 4 5]

[0 1 2 3 4 5]

Explanation:

"arr1=np.array([0, 1, 2, 3, 4, 5])" creates a NumPy array arr1.

"arr2 = np.arange(0, 6)" creates a NumPy array arr2.

Zero-Dimensional Array

A Zero-Dimensional array is called a scalar, its element is only a value.

The syntax to create a zero-dimensional array is:

```
myArray = np.array(value)
```

Example 1.4

```
import numpy as np
myArray = np.array(100)
print(myArray)
```

Output:

100

Explanation:

"np.array(100)" creates a zero-dimensional array with a value 100.

One-Dimensional Array

A One-Dimensional array contains multiple values.

The syntax to create a one-dimensional array is:

```
myArray = np.array([value1, value2, value3......])
```

Example 1.5

```
import numpy as np

myArray = np.array([0, 1, 2, 3, 4, 5])

print(myArray)
```

Output:

[0 1 2 3 4 5]

Explanation:

"np.array([0, 1, 2, 3, 4, 5])" creates a one-dimensional array.

The 1-d array only has one **[ ]**.

Two-Dimensional Array

A Two-Dimensional Array contains multiple one-dimensional arrays.

The syntax to create a two-dimensional array is:

```
myArray = np.array( [ [v1, v2, v3] , [v4, v5, v6] ] )
```

Example 1.6

```
import numpy as np
myArray = np.array([[0, 1, 2], [3, 4, 5]])
print(myArray)
```

Output:

[[0 1 2]

 [3 4 5]]

Explanation:

"np.array([[0, 1, 2], [3, 4, 5]])" creates a two-dimensional array.

The 2-d array has two [ ].

Three-Dimensional Array

A Three-Dimensional Array contains multiple two-dimensional arrays.

The syntax to create a three-dimensional array is:

myArr = np.array([[[v1, v2, v3] , [v4, v5, v6], [v7, v8, v9]]])

Example 1.7

```
import numpy as np
myArr = np.array([[[0,1,2], [3,4,5], [6,7,8]]])
print(myArr)
```

Output:

[[[0 1 2]

  [3 4 5]

  [6 7 8]]]

Explanation:

"**np.array([[[0,1,2], [3,4,5], [6,7,8]]])**" creates a three-dimensional array.

The 3-d array has three **[ ]**.

Hour 2

High Dimension Array

The syntax to define a higher dimension array is:

```
ndmin = number
```

The "number" means how many dimensions in an array.

Example 2.1

```
import numpy as np
arr3 = np.array([ 0, 1, 2, 3 ], ndmin=3)    # define 3d array
arr4 = np.array([ 0, 1, 2, 3 ], ndmin=4)    # define 4d array
arr5 = np.array([ 0, 1, 2, 3 ], ndmin=5)    # define 5d array
print(arr3)
print(arr4)
print(arr5)
```

Output:

[[[0 1 2 3]]]

[[[[0 1 2 3]]]]

[[[[[0 1 2 3]]]]]

Explanation:

"Ndmin = number" can define a higher dimension array.

The Number of Dimension

The syntax to check the how many dimensions of an array is:

```
myArray.ndim
```

Example 2.2

```
import numpy as np
arr0 = np.array(100)      # 0d array
arr1 = np.array([0, 1, 2, 3, 4, 5])      # 1d array
arr2 = np.array([[0, 1, 2], [3, 4, 5,]])      # 2d array
arr3 = np.array([[[0,1,2], [3,4,5], [6,7,8]]])      # 3d array
print(arr0.ndim)
print(arr1.ndim)
print(arr2.ndim)
print(arr3.ndim)
```

Output:

0

1

2

3

Explanation:

"myArray.ndim" can check the number of dimensions in an array.

Access the Array Element

We can access the array element by using array index. Each array element has its own index. The array index begins with 0.

The syntax to access an array element is:

```
myArray[index]
```

Example 2.3

```
import numpy as np

myArray = np.array([10, 11, 12, 13, 14])

print(myArray[0])

print(myArray[3])
```

Output:

10
13

Explanation:

The array index begins with 0.

"**myArray[0]**" accesses the number zero element.

"**myArray[3]**" accesses the number three element.

Calculate the Element Values

We can calculate the element's value of an array by using the array index.

Example 2.4

```
import numpy as np

myArray = np.array([10, 11, 12, 13, 14])

print(myArray[0] + myArray[3])

print(myArray[1] * myArray[2])
```

Output:

23

132

Explanation:

"**myArray[0] + myArray[3]**" means "10+23", returns 23

"**myArray[1] * myArray[2]**" means "11*12", returns 132

We can also calculate the element's value with subtraction or division.

Access Two-Dimensional Array

We can access a two-dimensional array by index.

A two-dimensional array contains multiple rows and columns.

The syntax to access a 2-d array with rows and columns is:

```
myArray[ row, col ]
```

Example 2.5

```
import numpy as np
arr = np.array([[10,11,12,13,14], [15,16,17,18,19]])
print ('The value in row 0 and col 3 is: ', arr[0,3])
print ('The value in row 1 and col 2 is: ', arr[1,2])
```

Output:

The value in row 0 and col 3 is: 13

The value in row 1 and col 2 is: 17

Explanation:

The array index begins with 0. We access "arr" by index:

"**arr[0, 3]**" returns the value in row 0 and col 3.

"**arr[1, 2]**" returns the value in row 1 and col 2.

Last Index

We can use "-1" to represent the last index.

```
myArray[-1, -1]      # access the last row and the last col
```

Example 2.6

```
import numpy as np

arr = np.array([[10,11,12,13,14], [15,16,17,18,19]])

print ('The value in row 0 and the last col is: ', arr[0,-1])

print ('The value in the last row and col 2 is: ', arr[-1,2])

print ('The value in the last row & the last col is: ', arr[-1,-1])
```

Output:

The value in row 0 and the last col is: 14

The value in the last row and col 2 is: 17

The value in the last row & the last col is: 19

Explanation:

"arr[-1,-1]" can access the element in the last row & the last col.

NumPy Slicing

We can get part of the elements from one index to another index.

[start : end : step]

The value of "end" is the index-1.

The default value of "step" is 1.

Example 2.7

```
import numpy as np
arr = np.array([10, 11, 12, 13, 14, 15, 16, 17, 18])
print(arr[ 2:7:2 ])
print(arr[ 2:7 ])
```

Output:

[12 14 16]

[12 13 14 15 16]

Explanation:

Note: The value of "end" is the index-1.

"[2:7:2])" returns the elements from the index2 to index7-1, step value is 2.

Slicing by Default

In [start : end : step], the default values are:

The default value of "start" is the first index.

The default value of "end" is the last index.

The default value of "step" is 1

Example 2.8

```
import numpy as np

arr = np.array([10, 11, 12, 13, 14, 15, 16, 17, 18])

print(arr[ :5])

print(arr[5: ])
```

Output:

[10 11 12 13 14]

[15 16 17 18]

Explanation:

"**arr[:5]**" returns elements from the first index to index5-1.

"**arr[5:]**" returns elements from index5 to the last index.

Negative Slicing

Negative Slicing means to refer to the index from the end.

```
arr[ -index1: -index2 ]
```

Access the elements from -index1 to -index2-1, refer to the index from the end.

Example 2.9

```
import numpy as np
arr = np.array([10, 11, 12, 13, 14, 15, 16, 17, 18])
print(arr[-5 : -2])
print(arr[-7 : -3])
```

Output:

[14 15 16]

[12 13 14 15]

Explanation:

Negative slicing refers to the index from the end.

"**arr[-5 : -2]**" returns the elements from -index5 to -index2-1.

"**arr[-7 : -3]**" returns the elements from -index7 to -index3-1.

2-D Array Slicing (1)

The 1st syntax to slice a 2-d array is:

myArray[row1: row2, col1: col2]

"myArray[row1: row2, col1: col2]" accesses the elements from row1 to row2-1, and from col1 to col2-1.

Example 2.10

```
import numpy as np
arr = np.array([[10, 11, 12, 13, 14], [15,16,17,18,19]])
print(arr[0:2, 2:4])
```

Output:

[[12 13]

 [17 18]]

Explanation:

"arr[0:2, 2:4]" returns the elements from row0 to row2-1, and from col2 to col4-1.

2-D Array Slicing (2)

The 2nd syntax to slice a 2-d array is:

myArray[row, col1:col2]

"myArray[row, col1:col2] "accesses the elements in the specified row, and from col1 to col2-1.

Example 2.11

```
import numpy as np
arr = np.array([[10, 11, 12, 13, 14], [15,16,17,18,19]])
print(arr[0, 1:4])
print(arr[1, 2:4])
```

Output:

[11 12 13]

[17 18]

Explanation:

"**arr[0, 1:4]**" returns the elements in the row0, from col1 to col4-1.

"**arr[1, 2:4]**" returns the elements in the row1, from col2 to col4-1.

2-D Array Slicing (3)

The 3rd syntax to slice a 2-d array is:

myArray[row1: row2, col]

"myArray[row1: row2, col]" accesses the elements from row1 to row2-1, and in the specified col.

Example 2.12

```
import numpy as np
arr = np.array([[10, 11, 12, 13, 14], [15,16,17,18,19]])
print(arr[0:2, 2])
print(arr[0:1, 3])
```

Output:

[12 17]

[13]

Explanation:

"arr[0:2, 2]" returns the elements from row0 to row2-1, in the col2.

"arr[0:1, 3]" returns the elements from row0 to row1-1, in the col3.

Hour 3

NumPy Data Type

NumPy data type can be described by one character.

Character	Data Type
i	integer or int64
b	boolean
u	unsigned
f	float
c	complex
m	timedelta
>	more than characters (bit-endian byte order)
<	less than characters (little-endian byte order)
		not applicable to use the byte order
M	datetime
O	object
S	string
U	unicode
V	void

Type Code

Each NumPy Data Type has its own type code. For example:

The type code of the int64 is "i8", the type code of the string is "S" or "|S"

Type	Type code
int8, uint8	i1, u1
int16, uint16	i2, u2
int32, uint32	i4, u4
int64, uint64	i8, u8
float16	f2
float32	f4 or f
float64	f8 or d
float128	f16 or g
complex64, complex128, complex256	c8, c16, c32
bool	?
object	0
string_	S or |S
unicode_	U

Check Data Type

The syntax to check the data type of an array is:

```
myArray.dtype
```

Example 3.1

```
import numpy as np
arr1 = np.array([10, 11, 12, 13])
print(arr1.dtype)
arr2 = np.array(['Matlab','in', '8', 'Hours'])
print(arr2.dtype)
```

Output:

int64

<U6

Explanation:

"arr1.dtype" and "arr2.dtype" returns the data type of the arrays.

"int64" means the integer type with 64 bits.

"<U6" means that each unsigned string has no more than six characters in this array (Matlab in 8 Hours).

"<" is a symbol of the little-endian byte order.

Set a String Array

The syntax to set up a string type of an array is:

```
dtype = 'S'
```

Example 3.2

```
import numpy as np
myArr = np.array([10, 20, 30, 40], dtype='S')
print(myArr.dtype)
```

Output:

|S2

Explanation:

"dtype='S'" sets the data type of the array to be a string.

"|"symbol means that it's not applicable to use the byte order symbol here.

"S2" means that the array data type is String, the size of the each element is 2 bytes.

Set an Int Array

The syntax to set up an int type of an array is:

```
dtype = ' i1 / i2 / i4 / i8 '
```

Example 3.3

```
import numpy as np

myArr = np.array([10, 11, 12, 13], dtype='i2')

print(myArr.dtype)
```

Output:

int16

Explanation:

"dtype='i2'" sets up the int16 as the data type of the array.

"i2" is the type code of the int16.

Convert Integer Type

The syntax to convert the data type of an array is:

```
myArr.astype('data_type')
```

Example 3.4

```
import numpy as np

myArr = np.array([0.99, 1.99, 2.99, 3.99])

arr = myArr.astype('i')

print(arr)

print(arr.dtype)
```

Output:

```
[0 1 2 3]
int32
```

Explanation:

"astype('i')" converts the array to integer type.

"int32" indicates that the data type of the array has been converted to integer type.

Convert Bool Type

The syntax to convert the data type of an array is:

```
myArr.astype('data_type')
```

Example 3.5

```
import numpy as np

myArr = np.array([0, 1, 2, 3])

arr = myArr.astype(bool)

print(arr)

print(arr.dtype)
```

Output:

```
[False  True  True  True]
bool
```

Explanation:

"**astype(bool)**" converts the array to boolean type.

"bool" indicates that the data type of the array has been converted to boolean type.

Copy an Array

The syntax to copy an array is:

```
array2 = array1.copy()
```

Example 3.6

```
import numpy as np
arr1 = np.array([0, 1, 2, 3, 4])   # arr1 is an original array
arr2 = arr1.copy()        # arr2 is a new array
arr2[0] = 100
print(arr1)
print(arr2)
```

Output:

[0 1 2 3 4]

[100 1 2 3 4]

Explanation:

"**arr2 = arr1.copy()**" copies arr1 to arr2.

Changing arr2 will not affect arr1.

Changing arr1 will not affect arr2.

The View of Array

The syntax to create a view of an array is:

```
array2 = array1.view()
```

Example 3.7

```
import numpy as np
arr1 = np.array([0, 1, 2, 3, 4])    # arr1 is an original array
arr2 = arr1.view()        # arr2 is a view
arr2[0] = 100
print(arr1)
print(arr2)
```

Output:

[100 1 2 3 4]

[100 1 2 3 4]

Explanation:

"**arr2 = arr1.view()**" creates a view arr2 from arr1.

Changing arr2 will affect arr1.

Changing arr1 will affect arr2.

Check Correlation

"**array.base**" can check the correlation of the new array and the old array.

If the newArray is copied from the oldArray, then the "**newArray.base**" will return "None".

If the newArray is the view of the oldArray, then the "**newArray.base**" will return a new array.

Example 3.8

```
import numpy as np
myArr = np.array([0, 1, 2, 3, 4])
copyArr = myArr.copy()
viewArr = myArr.view()
print(copyArr.base)
print(viewArr.base)
```

Output:

None

[0 1 2 3 4]

Explanation:

"**array.base**" can check the correlation of newArray & oldArray.

Array Shape (1)

Array Shape means how many row elements and how many column elements in an array.

The syntax to get the shape of an array is:

```
array.shape
```

Example 3.9

```
import numpy as np
myArr = np.array([[0,1,2,3],[4,5,6,7],[2,4,6,8]])
print(myArr.shape)
```

Output:

(3, 4)

Explanation:

"**myArr.shape**" returns a (3, 4), which indicates that the "myArr" has 3 rows of elements and 4 columns of elements.

Array Shape (2)

Let's study one more example.

Example 3.10

```
import numpy as np
myArr = np.array([1, 2, 3, 4, 5], ndmin=2)
print(myArr)
print('The array shape is:', myArr.shape)
```

Output:

[[1 2 3 4 5]]

The array shape is: (1, 5)

Explanation:

"ndmin=2" sets up a 2 dimensions array.

"myArr.shape" returns the shape (1, 5), which means myArr contains 1 row of elements and 5 columns of elements.

Hour 4

Reshape From 1D to 2D

Array Reshape means modifying the shape of an array.

The syntax to reshape from the 1-d array to the 2-d array is:

```
2dArray = 1dArray.reshape(rows, columns)
```

Example 4.1

```
import numpy as np
myArr = np.array([0, 1, 2, 3, 4, 5, 6, 7, 8, 9, 10, 11])
newArr = myArr.reshape(3, 4)
print(newArr)
```

Output:

[[0 1 2 3]

 [4 5 6 7]

 [8 9 10 11]]

Explanation:

"myArr.reshape(3, 4)" reshapes from 1-d array to 2-d array, which contains 3 rows of elements and 4 columns of elements.

Reshape From 2D to 3D

The syntax to reshape from the 1-d array to the 3-d array is:

```
3dArray = 1dArray.reshape( layers, rows, columns )
```

The parameter "layers" means that the 3-d array will contain the number of arrays.

Example 4.2

```
import numpy as np

myArr = np.array([0, 1, 2, 3, 4, 5, 6, 7, 8, 9, 10, 11])

newArr = myArr.reshape(2, 2, 3)

print(newArr)
```

Output:

```
[[[ 0  1  2]
  [ 3  4  5]]
 [[ 6  7  8]
  [ 9 10 11]]]
```

Explanation:

The result is a 3-d array, which contains two 2-d arrays with 2 rows of elements and 3 columns of elements.

Reshape Requirement

The requirement of the array reshape is:

> The number of elements in the original array must equal the product of the dimensions.

Example 4.3

Given arr([1,2,3,4,5,6,7,8,9,10,11,12]) has total **12** elements:

When it is reshaped to a 2-d array: we can use:

arr.reshape(2, 6)   # 2*6=**12**

arr.reshape(3, 4)   # 3*4=**12**

arr.reshape(4, 3)   # 4*3=**12**

......

When it is reshaped to a 3-d array: we can use:

arr.reshape(1, 3, 4)   # 1*3*4=**12**

arr.reshape(2, 3, 2)   # 2*3*2=**12**

arr.reshape(3, 2, 2)   # 3*2*2=**12**

......

If the product of the dimensions is not equal to the number of elements in the original array, the reshape will cause an error.

Unknown Dimension

If we do not specify an exact number for one of the dimensions in the reshape method, we can use "**-1**" as a parameter. NumPy will calculate this number automatically. Three syntaxes are:

```
arr.reshape( -1, rows, columns )
```
```
arr.reshape( layer, -1, columns )
```
```
arr.reshape( layer, rows, -1 )
```

Example 4.4

```
import numpy as np
myArr = np.array([1, 2, 3, 4, 5, 6, 7, 8, 9, 10, 11, 12])
newArr = myArr.reshape( -1, 2, 3 )
print(newArr)
```

Output:

```
[[[ 1  2  3]
  [ 4  5  6]]
 [[ 7  8  9]
  [10 11 12]]]
```

Explanation:

"**reshape(-1, 2, 3)**" sets up an unknown dimension, NumPy can calculate the dimensions automatically.

Flattening Array

Flattening Array means that reshape the multiple dimensional arrays to a 1-d array.

The syntax to reshape an array into a 1-d array is:

myArr.reshape(-1)

Example 4.5

```
import numpy as np

myArr = np.array([[1,2,3], [4,5,6], [7,8,9]])

newArr = myArr.reshape(-1)

print(newArr)
```

Output:

[1 2 3 4 5 6 7 8 9]

Explanation:

"myArr" is a 2-d array.

"myArr.reshape(-1)" uses the parameter "-1" to reshape the 2-d array into a 1-d array.

Iterating 1-d Array

The syntax to iterate through all elements in a 1-d array is:

```
for num in myArray
```

Example 4.6

```
import numpy as np

myArr = np.array([10, 11, 12])

for num in myArr:
  print(num)
```

Output:

10

11

12

Explanation:

myArr is a 1-d array.

"for n in myArr:" iterates through each element in myArr, and stores each element value in variable "num".

Iterating 2-d Array

The syntax to iterate through all elements in a 2-d array is:

```
for num in myArray
```

Example 4.7

```
import numpy as np
myArr = np.array([[10, 11, 12], [13, 14, 15]])
for num in myArr:
  print(num)
```

Output:

[10 11 12]

[13 14 15]

Explanation:

myArr is a 2-d array.

"for n in myArr:" iterates through each element in myArr, and stores each element value in variable "num".

Iterating 3-d Array

The syntax to iterate through all elements in a 3-d array is:

```
for num in myArray
```

Example 4.8

```
import numpy as np
myArr=np.array([[[10,11,12],[13,14,15]],[[16,17,18],[19,20,21]]])
for num in myArr:
  print(num)
```

Output:

[[10 11 12]

 [13 14 15]]

[[16 17 18]

 [19 20 21]]

Explanation:

myArr is a 3-d array.

"for n in myArr:" iterates through each element in myArr, and stores each element value in variable "num".

nditer()

To get each actual element value (scalar), we can use nditer() to iterate through all elements in the array. The syntax is:

```
nditer(myArray)
```

Example 4.9

```
import numpy as np
myArr = np.array([[10, 11, 12], [13, 14, 15]])
for num in np.nditer(myArr):     # myArr is a 2d array
  print(num)
```

Output:

10
11
12
13
14
15

Explanation:

"for num in np.nditer(myArr):" iterates through each element in myArr, and return each actual value (scalar) of the elements.

Example 4.10

```
import numpy as np
myArr=np.array([[[10,11,12],[13,14,15]],[[16,17,18],[19,20,21]]])
for num in np.nditer(myArr):      # myArr is a 3d array
  print(num)
```

Output:

10
11
12
13
14
15
16
17
18
19
20
21

Explanation:

"for num in np.nditer(myArr):" iterates through each element in myArr, and return each actual value (scalar) of the elements.

Iterating with Step Length

Iterating with step length is mainly used in the 2-d array.

The syntax of the step length is:

```
nditer( myArr[ :,: :step ] )
```

Example 4.11

```
import numpy as np
myArr = np.array([[10, 11, 12, 13], [14, 15, 16, 17]])
for num in np.nditer(myArr[:,: :2]):
  print(num)
```

Output:

10
12
14
16

Explanation:

"nditer(myArr[:,: :2])" sets up a step length, by which NumPy
Iterating through every scalar element of the array, each step
skips 1 element.

Enumerating the Array

We can specify a sequence number to each element in an array.

```
ndenumerate(myArray)
```

Example 4.12

```
import numpy as np

myArr = np.array([0, 1, 2, 3])

for id, num in np.ndenumerate(myArr):

  print(id, num)
```

Output:

(0,) 0

(1,) 1

(2,) 2

(3,) 3

Explanation:

"ndenumerate(myArr)" specifies the sequence number to each element in myArr.

Hour 5

Concatenating Arrays

Concatenating Arrays mean joining elements of two or more arrays into a single array.

The syntax to concatenate arrays is:

np.concatenate((array1, array2))

Example 5.1

```
import numpy as np

a1 = np.array([0, 1, 2])

a2 = np.array([3, 4, 5])

myArr = np.concatenate((a1, a2))

print(myArr)
```

Output:

[0 1 2 3 4 5]

Explanation:

"np.concatenate((a1, a2))" joins the elements in array1 and array2 into a single array.

Axis, a Big Issue

When concatenating two arrays, we will use a parameter "axis".

axis = 0   # join two arrays vertically

axis = 1   # join two arrays horizontally

Example 5.2

Assume that there are two 2-d arrays that will be concatenated:

Array1	Array2
[1, 2]	[5, 6]
[3, 4]	[7, 8]

When axis = 0

"axis = 0" means joining two arrays vertically.

The 1st item is [1,2], the 2nd item is [3,4], the 3rd item is [5,6], the 4th item is [7,8]. The result will be like: [1,2][3,4][5,6][7,8].

When axis = 1

"axis = 1" means joining two arrays horizontally.

The 1st item is [1,2], the 2nd item is [5,6], the 3rd item is [3,4], the 4th item is [7,8]. The result will be like: [1,2][5,6][3,4][7,8].

Concatenate Arrays (axis=0)

The 1st syntax to concatenate two arrays is:

```
np.concatenate((array1, array2), axis=0)
```

Example 5.3

```
import numpy as np

a1 = np.array([[11,12,13], [14,15,16]])

a2 = np.array([[21,22,23], [24,25,26]])

myArr = np.concatenate((a1, a2), axis=0)

print(myArr)
```

Output:

[[11 12 13]

 [14 15 16]

 [21 22 23]

 [24 25 26]]

Explanation:

"np.concatenate((a1, a2), **axis=0**)" joins two arrays **vertically**, because of the parameter "axis = 0".

Concatenate Arrays (axis=1)

The 2nd syntax to concatenate two arrays is:

```
np.concatenate((array1, array2), axis=1)
```

Example 5.4

```
import numpy as np
a1 = np.array([[11,12,13], [14,15,16]])
a2 = np.array([[21,22,23], [24,25,26]])
myArr = np.concatenate((a1, a2), axis=1)
print(myArr)
```

Output:

[[11 12 13 21 22 23]

 [14 15 16 24 25 26]]

Explanation:

"np.concatenate((a1, a2), **axis=1**)" joins two arrays **horizontally**, because of the parameter "axis = 1".

Note: If axis is not explicitly specified, its default value is 0.

Stack Arrays (axis=0)

The stack() can join two arrays, but it joins two 1-d arrays to be one 2-d array, and joins two 2-d arrays to be one 3-d array.

The 1st syntax to stack two arrays is:

```
np.stack((array1, array2), axis=0)
```

Example 5.5

```
import numpy as np
a1 = np.array([[11,12,13], [14,15,16]])
a2 = np.array([[21,22,23], [24,25,26]])
myArr = np.stack((a1, a2), axis=0)
print(myArr)
```

Output:

```
[[[11 12 13]
  [14 15 16]]
 [[21 22 23]
  [24 25 26]]]
```

Explanation:

"np.stack((a1, a2), **axis=0**)" joins two arrays **vertically**, because of the parameter "axis = 0".

Stack Arrays (axis=1)

The stack() can join two arrays, but it joins two 1-d arrays to be one 2-d array, and joins two 2-d arrays to be one 3-d array.

The 2nd syntax to stack two arrays is:

```
np.stack((array1, array2), axis=1)
```

Example 5.6

```
import numpy as np
a1 = np.array([[11,12,13], [14,15,16]])
a2 = np.array([[21,22,23], [24,25,26]])
myArr = np.stack((a1, a2), axis=1)
print(myArr)
```

Output:

```
[[[11 12 13]
  [21 22 23]]
 [[14 15 16]
  [24 25 26]]]
```

Explanation:

"np.stack((a1, a2), **axis=1**)" joins two arrays **horizontally**, because of the parameter "axis = 1".

Join Arrays Vertically

The vstack() can join two arrays vertically. The syntax is:

```
np.vstack((array1, array2))
```

Example 5.7

```
import numpy as np

a1 = np.array([[11,12,13], [14,15,16]])

a2 = np.array([[21,22,23], [24,25,26]])

myArr = np.vstack((a1, a2))

print(myArr)
```

Output:

```
[[11 12 13]

 [14 15 16]

 [21 22 23]

 [24 25 26]]
```

Explanation:

"np.vstack((a1, a2))" joins two arrays vertically.

Join Arrays Horizontally

The hstack() can join two arrays horizontally. The syntax is:

```
np.hstack((array1, array2))
```

Example 5.8

```
import numpy as np

a1 = np.array([[11,12,13], [14,15,16]])

a2 = np.array([[21,22,23], [24,25,26]])

myArr = np.hstack((a1, a2))

print(myArr)
```

Output:

[[11 12 13 21 22 23]

 [14 15 16 24 25 26]]

Explanation:

"**np.hstack((a1, a2))**" joins two arrays horizontally.

Join 1d Arrays to be 3d Array

We can join two 1d arrays to be one 3d array. The syntax is:

```
np.dstack((array1,array2))
```

By default, "dstack()" join two arrays horizontally.

Example 5.9

```
import numpy as np

a1 = np.array([11,12,13])      # 1d array

a2 = np.array([14,15,16])      # 1d array

myArr = np.dstack((a1,a2))

print(myArr)
```

Output:

[[[11 14]

 [12 15]

 [13 16]]]

Explanation:

The result "myArr" is a 3d array.

np.dstack((a1,a2)) joins two 1d arrays to be one 3d array.

Join 2d Arrays to be 3d Array

We can join two 2d arrays to be one 3d array. The syntax is:

```
np.dstack((array1,array2))
```

By default, "dstack()" join two arrays horizontally.

Example 5.10

```
import numpy as np
a1 = np.array([[11],[12],[13]])    # 2d array
a2 = np.array([[14],[15],[16]])    # 2d array
myArr = np.dstack((a1,a2))
print(myArr)
```

Output:

[[[11 14]]

 [[12 15]]

 [[13 16]]]

Explanation:

The result "myArr" is a 3d array.

"np.dstack((a1,a2))" joins two 2d arrays to be one 3d array.

Sorting Number Array

The sort() can sort all elements of an array.

The syntax to sort a number array is:

```
np.sort(array)
```

Example 5.11

```
import numpy as np

myArr = np.array([[ 2, 0, 3, 1 ], [ 7, 5, 6, 4 ]])

print(np.sort(myArr))
```

Output:

```
[[ 0 1 2 3 ]
 [ 4 5 6 7 ]]
```

Explanation:

"np.sort(myArr)" sorts all number elements in myArr.

Sort String Array

The sort() can sort all elements of an array.

The syntax to sort a string array is:

```
np.sort(array)
```

Example 5.12

```
import numpy as np

myArr = np.array(['dove', 'buffalo', 'antilope','camel'])

print(np.sort(myArr))
```

Output:

['antilope' 'buffalo' 'camel' 'dove']

Explanation:

"np.sort(myArr)" sorts all string elements in myArr.

73

Hour 6

Split an Array

Splitting an Array means breaking one array into multiple arrays.

The syntax to split one array is:

array_split(array, number)

The parameter "number" means how many arrays will be split.

Example 6.1

```
import numpy as np
myArr = np.array([10, 20, 30, 40, 50, 60])
arr = np.array_split(myArr, 3)
print(arr)
```

Output:

[array([10, 20]), array([30, 40]), array([50, 60])]

Explanation:

"np.array_split(myArr, 3)" splits myArr into three arrays.

Split Less Elements

If the array element is not enough to split evenly, NumPy will adjust them automatically

Example 6.2

```
import numpy as np

myArr = np.array([10, 20, 30, 40, 50, 60])

arr = np.array_split(myArr, 4)

print(arr)
```

Output:

[array([10, 20]), array([30, 40]), array([50]), array([60])]

Explanation:

"np.array_split(myArr, 4)" splits myArr into 4 arrays, but last two arrays only have one element, because NumPy can automatically adjust them.

Access Split Array

We can access the arrays that have been split. The syntax is:

```
arr[index]      # arr is an array that has been split
```

Example 6.3

```python
import numpy as np
myArr = np.array([10, 20, 30, 40, 50, 60])
arr = np.array_split(myArr, 3)
print(arr)
print(arr[0])
print(arr[1])
print(arr[2])
```

Output:

[array([10, 20]), array([30, 40]), array([50, 60])]

[10 20]

[30 40]

[50 60]

Explanation:

"arr[0], arr[1], arr[2]" accesses the elements of three split arrays.

Split 2-D Arrays

The syntax to split one 2-d array is:

```
array_split( array, number )
```

The parameter "number" means how many arrays will be split.

Example 6.4

```
import numpy as np
myArr = np.array([[1, 2], [3, 4], [5, 6], [7, 8]])     # 2d array
arr = np.array_split(myArr, 2)
print(arr)
```

Output:

[array([[1, 2], [3, 4]]),

 array([[5, 6], [7, 8]])]

Explanation:

"np.array_split(myArr, 2)" splits myArr into two arrays.

Split Vertically

We can split an array vertically.

The syntax to split an array vertically is:

vsplit(array, number)

The parameter "number" means how many arrays will be split.

Example 6.5

```
import numpy as np

myArr = np.array([[1, 2], [3, 4], [5, 6], [7, 8]])    # 2d array

arr = np.vsplit(myArr, 2)

print(arr)
```

Output:

[array([[1, 2], [3, 4]]), array([[5, 6], [7, 8]])]

Explanation:

"np.vsplit(myArr, 2)" vertically splits myArr into 2 arrays.

Split Horizontally

We can split an array horizontally.

The syntax to split an array horizontally is:

```
hsplit(array, number)
```

The parameter "number" means how many arrays will be split.

Example 6.6

```
import numpy as np
myArr = np.array([[1, 2], [3, 4], [5, 6], [7, 8]])    # 2d array
arr = np.hsplit(myArr, 2)
print(arr)
```

Output:

[array([[1],[3],[5],[7]]),

  array([[2],[4],[6],[8]])]

Explanation:

"np.hsplit(myArr, 2)" horizontally splits myArr into 2 arrays.

Find Array Index

We can find out the matched indexes by the element value, and return a new array containing matched indexes.

The syntax to find out the matched indexes is:

```
where(array == value)
```

Example 6.7

```
import numpy as np

myArr = np.array([0, 3, 2, 3, 4, 5, 3])

arr = np.where(myArr == 3)

print(arr)
```

Output:

(array([1, 3, 6]),)

Explanation:

"np.where(myArr == 3)" finds out all indexes whose value is 3, and returns a new array whose elements are matched indexes, which also means that the value 3 appears at index 1, 3 and 6.

Where is Even/Odd Number?

We can find out the indexes where the even numbers or the odd numbers locate.

Example 6.8

```
import numpy as np
myArr = np.array([ 10, 55, 21, 62, 29, 75, 36, 98])
even = np.where(myArr%2==0)
print(even)
odd = np.where(myArr%2==1)
print(odd)
```

Output:

(array([0, 3, 6, 7]),)

(array([1, 2, 4, 5]),)

Explanation:

"where(myArr%2==0)" finds out the indexes where the even numbers locate.

"where(myArr%2==1)" finds out the indexes where the odd numbers locate.

Search Index in a Location

In a sorted array, we can search an index by using a value that is not in the current array. The syntax is:

```
searchsorted( array, value )
```

Example 6.9

```
import numpy as np
myArr = np.array([24, 35, 46, 57, 68])
arr1 = np.searchsorted(myArr, 45)
arr2 = np.searchsorted(myArr, 47)
print(arr1)
print(arr2)
```

Output:

2

3

Explanation:

"**searchsorted(myArr, 45)**" finds out the index whose value is 45. Although the original array has no 45, its index should be 2.

"**searchsorted(myArr, 47)**" finds out the index whose value is 47. Although the original array has no 47, its index should be 3.

Search More Indexes

We can search multiple indexes simultaneously.

The syntax to search multiple indexes is:

```
searchsorted( array, [v1, v2, v3,…] )
```

Example 6.10

```
import numpy as np
myArr = np.array([13, 24, 35, 46, 57, 68, 79])
arr = np.searchsorted(myArr, [15, 45, 65])
print(arr)
```

Output:

[1 3 5]

Explanation:

"**searchsorted(myArr, [15, 45, 65])**" searches three indexes according to three specified values at the same time.

Filter Array by Boolean

We can filter the elements of an array by using Boolean value.

If the value is true, the element will be shown.

If the value is false, the element will not be shown.

Example 6.11

```
import numpy as np

myArr = np.array([0, 1, 2, 3, 4, 5])

arr = myArr[[True, False, True, False, False, True]]

print(arr)
```

Output:

[0 2 5]

Explanation:

"myArr[[True, False, True, False, False, True]]" is a filter, which is a boolean list corresponding the indexes in the array. Only elements corresponding to a true value can be displayed.

Filter Array by Condition

We can filter the elements of an array by using a condition.

If the value meets the condition, the element will be shown.

If the value doesn't the condition, the element will not be shown.

Example 6.12

```
import numpy as np

myArr = np.array([0, 1, 2, 3, 4, 5])

filter = myArr >= 3     # return true if meet the condition

arr = myArr[filter]

print(filter)

print(arr)
```

Output:

[False False False True True True]

[3 4 5]

Explanation:

"**myArr >= 3**" sets up a condition, only the elements that meet this condition can be displayed.

Hour 7

NumPy Ufuncs

The "Ufuncs" means "Universal Functions", which actually are NumPy functions. "Ufuncs" are used to realize vectorization to run NumPy program fast. We can regard the "Ufuncs" as a NumPy built-in function.

Example 7.1

```
import numpy as np
list1 = [10, 20, 30, 40]
list2 = [80, 70, 60, 50]
list3 = np.add(list1, list2)
print(list3)
```

Output:

[90 90 90 90]

Explanation:

"add()" is a NumPy ufunc.

"np.add(list1, list2)" means that list1 adds list2.

Check NumPy ufunc

We can check a function if it is a NumPy ufunc.

```
type(np.function_name)
```

If the type() returns <class 'numpy.ufunc'>, the function is proved to be an ufunc.

Example 7.2

```
import numpy as np
print(type(np.add))
print(type(np.subtract))
print(type(np.multiply))
print(type(np.divide))
```

Output:

<class 'numpy.ufunc'>

<class 'numpy.ufunc'>

<class 'numpy.ufunc'>

<class 'numpy.ufunc'>

Explanation:

The result is <class 'numpy.ufunc'>, which proves that add(), subtract(), multiply() and divide() are the NumPy ufuncs.

Create My Own ufunc

The steps to create my own ufunc are as follows:

1. Define a normal and my own Python function.

2. Add this function to the NumPy ufunc library. The syntax is:

```
frompyfunc(myFunction, number1, number2)
```

"number1" means the number of input arrays.

"number2" means the number of output array.

Example 7.3

```
import numpy as np
def myMultiply(a, b):      # define my own function
   return a*b
myMultiply = np.frompyfunc(myMultiply, 2, 1)
print(myMultiply([0, 1, 2, 3, 4 ], [5, 6, 7, 8, 9]))
```

Output:

[0   6 14 24 36]

Explanation:

"np.frompyfunc(myMultiply, 2, 1)" adds myMultiply() to the NumPy ufunc library. Two input arrays, One output array.

Arithmetic ufunc

"Arithmetic ufunc" means add(), subtract(), multiply(), divide().

Example 7.4

```
import numpy as np
arr1 = np.array([10,20,30])
arr2 = np.array([1, 2, 3])
a = np.add(arr1, arr2)
s = np.subtract(arr1, arr2)
m = np.multiply(arr1, arr2)
d = np.divide(arr1, arr2)
print(a)
print(s)
print(m)
print(d)
```

Output:

```
[11 22 33]
[ 9 18 27]
[10 40 90]
[10. 10. 10.]
```

Explanation:

The above example is simple arithmetic calculations.

power(), mod(), remainder()

The power() function rises the value of array1 to the power of the values of array2.

The mod() and remainder() get the remainder from the values of array1 being divided by the values of array2.

Example 7.5

```
import numpy as np
arr1 = np.array([10,10,10])
arr2 = np.array([2, 3, 4])
p = np.power(arr1, arr2)
m = np.mod(arr1, arr2)
r = np.remainder(arr1, arr2)
print(p)
print(m)
print(r)
```

Output:

```
[100  1000  10000 ]
[ 0  1  2 ]
[ 0  1  2 ]
```

Explanation:

The above example is simple arithmetic calculations.

trunc() & fix()

"trunk() & fix()" removes the decimal and return a number nearest the zero. The syntaxes are as follows:

```
trunk([ float_numbers ])
fix([ float_numbers ])
```

Example 7.6

```
import numpy as np

t = np.trunc([-2.71828, 2.71828])

f = np.fix([-2.71828, 2.71828])

print(t)

print(f)
```

Output:

[-2. 2.]

[-2. 2.]

Explanation:

"trunc([-2.71828, 2.71828])" & **"fix([-2.71828, 2.71828])"** remove the decimal and returns a new floating number nearest zero.

around(), ceil(), floor()

About NumPy arithmetic functions around(), ceil(), and floor():

around() returns a value being rounded off.

ceil() returns a smallest integer greater than itself.

floor() returns a largest integer less than itself.

Example 7.7

```
import numpy as np
a = np.around(7.555, 2)    # "2" means two decimal places
c = np.ceil(7.555)
f = np.floor(7.555)
print(a)
print(c)
print(f)
```

Output:

7.56

8.0

7.0

Explanation:

There are resembling functions like these in Python.

log2(), log10(), log()

About NumPy arithmetic functions log2(), log10(), and log():

```
log2(array)      # perform log in base 2
log10(array)     # perform log in base 10
log(array)       # perform log in base e
```

Example 7.8

```
import numpy as np

arr = np.arange(1,4)      # the range is from 1 to 3

print(np.log2(arr))

print(np.log10(arr))

print(np.log(arr))
```

Output:

```
[0.    1.          1.5849625]
[0.    0.30103     0.47712125]
[0.    0.69314718  1.09861229]
```

Explanation:

log2(), log10() and log() respectively perform log in base2, in base10 and in base e.

Log in Any Base

If the log base is any value, we need to use "from math import log" at the beginning of the code. The syntax is:

```
from math import log
......
math.log(number, base)
```

Example 7.9

```
from math import log
import numpy as np
print( log(16, 4) )      # the base is 4
```

Output:

2.0

Explanation:

"from math import log" helps to compute the log in any base.

"log(16, 4)" is a log in base 4.

Sum of Arrays

We can get the sum of all element values in multiple arrays.

```
sum( [array1, array2, array3] )
```

Example 7.10

```
import numpy as np
a1 = np.array([10, 20, 30])
a2 = np.array([10, 20, 30])
a3 = np.array([10, 20, 30])
myArr = np.sum([a1, a2, a3])
print(myArr)
```

Output:

180

Explanation:

The sum of all element values in three arrays comes from 3*(10+20+30).

Sum & Axis=0

The parameter "axis=0" can make NumPy **vertically** sum up the element values in multiple arrays.

Example 7.11

```
import numpy as np

a1 = np.array([1, 2, 3])

a2 = np.array([4, 5, 6])

myArr = np.sum([a1, a2], axis=0)

print(myArr)
```

Output:

[5 7 9]

Explanation:

"np.sum([a1, a2], axis=0)" vertically sums up the element values in two arrays because of "axis=0".

Sum & Axis=1

The parameter "axis=1" can make NumPy **horizontally** sum up the element values in multiple arrays.

Example 7.12

```
import numpy as np

a1 = np.array([1, 2, 3])

a2 = np.array([4, 5, 6])

myArr = np.sum([a1, a2], axis=1)

print(myArr)
```

Output:

[6 15]

Explanation:

np.sum([a1, a2], axis=1)" horizontally sums up the element values in two arrays because of "axis=1."

Hour 8

Cumulative Sum

"Cumulative Sum" is a special addition, it operates like this:

(1) (1+2) (1+2+3) (1+2+3+4) (1+2+3+4+5)......

The syntax of cumulative sum is:

cumsum(array)

Example 8.1

```
import numpy as np
myArr = np.array([10, 20, 30, 40])
arr = np.cumsum(myArr)
print(arr)
```

Output:

[10 30 60 100]

Explanation:

"**np.cumsum(myArr)**" adds each element cumulatively.

The calculating process is as follows:

[(10) (10+20) (10+20+30) (10+20+30+40)]

Difference of Array

The syntax to get the difference of an array is:

```
diff(myArr)
```

The calculating rule is: "nextElement – previousElement"

E.g. Given an array [1, 3, 8], we can get the difference in this way:

3-1=2, 8-3=5, the final result is [2 5].

Example 8.2

```
import numpy as np
myArr = np.array([2, 5, 6, 8])
arr = np.diff(myArr)
print(arr)
```

Output:

[3 1 2]

Explanation:

"np.diff(myArr)" returns the differences of myArr.

The calculating process is: 5-2=3, 6-5=1, 8-6=2.

The result is [3 1 2].

Once More Difference

The syntax to repeatedly get the difference is:

```
diff(myArr, n = number)
```

The parameter "number" is the number of times to repeat.

E.g. Given an array [1, 3, 8], **n=2.** we get difference in this way:

3-1=2, 8-3=5, returns [2 5]. Then, 5-2=3, the final result is [3]

Example 8.3

```
import numpy as np

myArr = np.array([2, 5, 6, 8])

arr = np.diff(myArr, n=2)

print(arr)
```

Output:

[-2   1]

Explanation:

"diff(myArr, n=2)" returns the differences of myArr two times.

The calculating process is: 5-2=3, 6-5=1, 8-6=2, returns [3 1 2].

Then, 1-3=-2, 2-1=1. The result is [-2   1].

Product of an Array

The syntax to get the product of all element values in an array is:

```
prod(array)
```

Example 8.4

```
import numpy as np
myArr = np.array([10, 20, 30, 40])
num = np.prod(myArr)        # 10*20*30*40
print(num)
```

Output:

240000

Explanation:

"np.prod(myArr)" returns the product of all element values in
myArr.

The calculating process is as follows:

240000 = 10x20x30x40

Product of Arrays

We can get the product of all element values in more than one array. The syntax is:

```
product = product1 * product2 * product3……
```

Example 8.5

```
import numpy as np
a1 = np.array([1, 2, 3])
a2 = np.array([4, 5, 6])
num = np.prod([a1, a2])     # 1*2*3*4*5*6
print(num)
```

Output:

720

Explanation:

"**np.prod([a1, a2])**" returns the product of all element values in a1 and a2.

The calculating process is as follows:

720 = 1*2*3*4*5*6

Product & Axis=0

The parameter "axis=0" can make NumPy **vertically** multiply the element values in multiple arrays.

Example 8.6

```
import numpy as np
a1 = np.array([1, 2, 3])
a2 = np.array([4, 5, 6])
myArr = np.prod([a1, a2], axis=0)
print(myArr)
```

Output:

[4 10 18]

Explanation:

"np.prod([a1, a2], axis=0)" vertically multiplies the element values in two arrays because of "axis=0".

Product & Axis=1

The parameter "axis=1" can make NumPy **horizontally** multiply the element values in multiple arrays.

Example 8.7

```
import numpy as np

a1 = np.array([1, 2, 3])

a2 = np.array([4, 5, 6])

myArr = np.prod([a1, a2], axis=1)

print(myArr)
```

Output:

[6 120]

Explanation:

"np.prod([a1, a2], axis=1)" horizontally multiplies the element values in two arrays because of "axis=1."

Cumulative Product

"Cumulative Product" is a special multiplication, It operates like this: (1) (1x2) (1x2x3) (1x2x3x4) (1x2x3x4x5)......

The syntax of cumulative product is:

```
cumprod(array)
```

Example 8.8

```
import numpy as np

myArr = np.array([1, 2, 3, 4])

arr = np.cumprod(myArr)

print(arr)
```

Output:

[1   2   6   24]

Explanation:

"**np.cumprod(myArr)**" multiplies each element cumulatively.

The calculating process is as follows:

[(1) (1X2) (1X2X3) (1X2X3X4)]

Quotient of Array

The syntax to get the quotients and the remainder of an array is:

```
divmod( array, divisor)
```

Example 8.9

```
import numpy as np
arr = np.arange(2,7)      # create an arr[ 2,3,4,5,6 ]
print(divmod(arr, 2))
```

Output:

(array([1, 1, 2, 2, 3]), array([0, 1, 0, 1, 0]))

Explanation:

"**divmod(arr, 2)**" returns the quotient and the remainder of an array.

"np.arange(2,7)" creates an array arr[2,3,4,5,6]

The calculating process is as follows:

[2,3,4,5,6] / 2 returns:

The quotient is [1, 1, 2, 2, 3]

The remainder is [0, 1, 0, 1, 0]

Lowest Common Multiple

Lowest Common Multiple (LCM) is the minimum number that is a common multiple of all elements in an array.

The syntax to get an LCM is:

```
lcm.reduce(array)
```

Example 8.10

```
import numpy as np

myArr = np.array([2, 5, 8])

num = np.lcm.reduce(myArr)

print(num)
```

Output:

40

Explanation:

"**lcm.reduce(myArr)**" returns an LCM 40.

The calculating process is as follows:

2x20=40, 5x8=40, 8x6=40.

Greatest Common Divisor

Greatest Common Divisor (GCD) is the maximum number that is a common factor of all elements in an array.

The syntax to get a GCD is:

```
gcd.reduce(array)
```

Example 8.11

```
import numpy as np

myArr = np.array([12, 6, 21, 9, 24])

num = np.gcd.reduce(myArr)

print(num)
```

Output:

3

Explanation:

"**gcd.reduce(myArr)**" returns a GCD 3.

The calculating process is as follows:

12/3=4, 6/3=2, 21/3=7, 9/3=3, 24/3=8.

Rearrange the Array

Two methods can randomly rearrange the element sequence of an array:

```
random.permutation(array)
random.shuffle(array)
```

The difference of two functions is: "permutation()" only changes the copy of the array. "shuffle()"changes the original array.

Example 8.12

```
from numpy import random
import numpy as np
myArr = np.array([1, 2, 3, 4, 5])
arr = random.permutation(myArr)
print(arr)
random.shuffle(myArr)
print(myArr)
```

Output:

```
[ 2  5  3  1  4 ]
[ 3  1  4  5  2 ]
```

Explanation: permutation() and shuffle() can randomly rearrange the element sequence of an array.

Numpy

Q & A

Questions

Please fill in the correct answer:

01.

```
import numpy as np
arr1 = np.array([0, 1, 2, 3, 4, 5])
print(arr1)
arr2 = np.fill-in( 0, 6 )      # create an array.
print(arr2)
```

A. rearrange

B. arrange

C. range

D. arange

02.

```
import numpy as np
arr3 = np.array([ 0, 1, 2, 3 ], fill in=3)     # define 3d array
print(arr3)
```

A. array

B. ndmin

C. npmin

D. admin

03.

```
import numpy as np

arr = np.array([10, 11, 12, 13])

print(arr.fill in)    # check the data type of the array
```

A. datatype

B. checktype

C. dtype

D. type

04.

```
import numpy as np

myArr = np.array([1, 2, 3, 4, 5, 6, 7, 8, 9, 10, 11, 12])

newArr = myArr.reshape( fill in, 2, 3 )
# sets up unknown dimension

print(newArr)
```

A. -1   B. 0   C. 1   D. 2

05.

```
import numpy as np

a1 = np.array([0, 1, 2])

a2 = np.array([3, 4, 5])

myArr = np.fill in((a1, a2))    # join two arrays
```

```
print(myArr)
```

A. join

B. connect

C. concat

D. concatenate

06.

```
import numpy as np
myArr = np.array([10, 20, 30, 40, 50, 60])
arr = np.fill in(myArr, 3)      # split an array
print(arr)
```

A. split

B. arraysplit

C. array_split

D. array-split

07.

```
import numpy as np
def myMultiply(a, b):      # define my own function
  return a*b
myMultiply = np.fill in(myMultiply, 2, 1)
print(myMultiply([0, 1, 2, 3, 4 ], [5, 6, 7, 8, 9]))
```

A. frompyfunc

B. ufunc

C. formpyfunc

D. ufuncs

08.

import numpy as np

myArr = np.array([10, 20, 30, 40])

arr = **np.fill in(myArr)**   # get the cumulative sum

print(arr)

A. cumulativesum

B. cumulatisum

C. cumulsum

D. cumsum

09.

What is the output based on the following code?

import numpy as np

arr = np.array([[10,11,12,13,14], [15,16,17,18,19]])

print (arr[-1,2])

A. 16   B. 17   C.18   D. 19

10.

What is the output based on the following code?

```
import numpy as np

myArr = np.array([10, 11, 12, 13], dtype='i2')

print(myArr.dtype)
```

A. int2

B. int8

C. int16

D. int32

11.

How many dimensional arrays will return based on the following code?

```
import numpy as np

myArr = np.array([0, 1, 2, 3, 4, 5, 6, 7, 8, 9, 10, 11])

newArr = myArr.reshape(2, 2, 3)

print(newArr)
```

A. 1d array

B. 2d array

C. 3d array

D. 4d array

12.

```
import numpy as np

a1 = np.array([[11,12,13], [14,15,16]])
```

```
a2 = np.array([[21,22,23], [24,25,26]])

myArr = np.stack((a1, a2), fill in)     # stack vertically

print(myArr)
```

A. axis = 0

B. axis = 1

C. axis = v

D. axis = h

13.

What is the output based on the following code?

```
import numpy as np

myArr = np.array([10, 20, 30, 40, 50, 60])

arr = np.array_split(myArr, 3)

print(arr[1])
```

A. [0 10]

B. [10 20]

C. [30 40]

D. [50 60]

14.

```
import numpy as np

t = np.fill in([-2.71828, 2.71828])     # remove the decimal

print(t)
```

A. trim

B. around

C. round

D. trunk

15.

```
import numpy as np

myArr = np.array([2, 5, 6, 8])

arr = np.fill in(myArr)

print(arr)
```

A. difference

B. diff

C. subtract

D. sub

16.

What is the output based on the following code?

```
import numpy as np

arr = np.array([10, 11, 12, 13, 14, 15, 16, 17, 18])

print(arr[ 2:7:2 ])
```

A. [12 14 16]

B. [11 13 15]

C. [13 15 17]

D. [12 13 14 15 16]

17.

```
import numpy as np

myArr = np.array([0, 1, 2, 3])

arr = myArr.fill in(bool)    # convert to bool type

print(arr)

print(arr.dtype)
```

A. convert

B. boolean

C. astype

D. type

18.

```
import numpy as np

myArr = np.array([[1,2,3], [4,5,6], [7,8,9]])

newArr = myArr.reshape(fill in)

# flatten 2d array to 1d array

print(newArr)
```

A. -1   B. 0   C. 1   D. 2

19.

```
import numpy as np
```

```
a1 = np.array([[11,12,13], [14,15,16]])

a2 = np.array([[21,22,23], [24,25,26]])

myArr = np.fill in((a1, a2))     # stack two arrays horizontally

print(myArr)
```

A. stackhorizon

B. shorizon

C. horizonstack

D. hstack

20.

```
import numpy as np
myArr = np.array([0, 3, 2, 3, 4, 5, 3])
arr = np.fill in(myArr == 3)     # finds array index
print(arr)
```

A. find

B. search

C. where

D. seek

21.

What is the output based on the following code?

```
import numpy as np
a1 = np.array([10, 20, 30])
```

```
a2 = np.array([10, 20, 30])

a3 = np.array([10, 20, 30])

myArr = np.sum([a1, a2, a3])

print(myArr)
```

A. [30   60   90]

B. [60, 60, 60]

C. [10, 20, 30] [10, 20, 30] [10, 20, 30]

D. 180

22.

What is the output based on the following code?

```
import numpy as np

myArr = np.array([2, 5, 6, 8])

arr = np.diff(myArr, n=2)

print(arr)
```

A. [-1   2]

B. [-2   1]

C. [-3   0]

D. [-1   3]

23.

```
import numpy as np

myArr = np.array([0, 1, 2, 3, 4])
```

```
copyArr = myArr.copy()
```

print(**copyArr.fill in**)   # check correlation

A. correlation

B. relation

C. base

D. association

24.

```
import numpy as np
myArr = np.array([[10, 11, 12], [13, 14, 15]])
```

for num in np.fill in(myArr):   # iterate through the array

  print(num)

A. iterate

B. while

C. foreach

D. nditer

Answers

01. D	09. B	17. C
02. B	10. C	18. A
03. C	11. C	19. D
04. A	12. A	20. C
05. D	13. C	21. D
06. C	14. D	22. B
07. A	15. B	23. C
08. D	16. A	24. D

Recommended Books by Ray Yao

(Each Cheat Sheet contains more than 300 examples, more than 300 outputs, and more than 300 explanations.)

Paperback Books by Ray Yao

C# Cheat Sheet

C++ Cheat Sheet

Java Cheat Sheet

JavaScript Cheat Sheet

Php MySql Cheat Sheet

Python Cheat Sheet

Html Css Cheat Sheet

Linux Command Line

C# 100 Q & A

C++ 100 Q & A

Java 100 Q & A

JavaScript 100 Q & A

Php MySql 100 Q & A

Python 100 Q & A

Html Css 100 Q & A

Linux 100 Q & A

C# Examples

C++ Examples

Java Examples

JavaScript Examples

Php MySql Examples

Python Examples

Html Css Examples

Shell Scriptng Examples

Advanced C++ in 8 hours

Advanced Java in 8 hours

AngularJs in 8 hours

C# programming

C++ programming

Dart in 8 hours

Django in 8 hours

Erlang in 8 hours

Git Github in 8 hours

Golang in 8 hours

Google Sheets in 8 hours

Haskell in 8 hours

Html Css programming

Java programming

JavaScript programming

Made in United States
Troutdale, OR
12/30/2024

27434902R00073